To

The Pocketbook of Shortcut Keys for Microsoft Office

Enjoy!

Steve

Published by James Grundy 3 Harper Close Macclesfield
Cheshire SK11 7QG

ISBN
978-0-9553775-1-8

A catalogue record of this book is available from the British
Library.

Shortcut keys compiled and edited by Steve Walsh
Book cover design by
Jason Lawton 1012 Creative Vision

Printed in the UK by Think Ink

This book is a 2009 First Edition

Online ordering available at our website
www.technopocketbooks.com

CONTENTS

CONTENTS

Introduction

The humble keyboard shortcut is one of the most productive tools in your arsenal if you are a regular computer user. Shortcut keys can be used everywhere. Almost every program has some support for shortcut keys. In fact, you've probably seen them but didn't realize how effective they could be!

The Pocketbook of Shortcut Keys will teach you the most simple but also the most effective keyboard shortcuts that anyone who uses a computer with Microsoft Office Suite Applications installed can benefit from. Try them out and get an understanding of what they do and then use them till they become habits. Eventually it will become second nature and the time you spend in learning shortcut keys will be paid back many times.

It is easy and fast to learn the shortcut keys you need. There are a huge amount of shortcut keys available for many of the most common programs. Furthermore, as you begin to work with shortcut keys you will notice that several applications share the same shortcut keys making it easier for you to apply them when using different programs.

Start using shortcut keys now and you will be amazed at how much time you will save.

Shortcut Keys

A shortcut key (or keyboard shortcut) is a set of keys pressed at the same time that activates a program command directly as an alternative to activating the command through the program menus. The de facto standard for listing a shortcut is listing the *modifier key*, *a plus symbol*, and the single letter *action key*. This standard is used throughout this book. For example **Ctrl + V** is the shortcut key for the Paste Command. Here, the **Ctrl key** is called the *modifier key* and **V key** is the *action key*.

The other common modifier keys are **Alt**, and **Shift**. Typically, the Shift key is used in conjunction with either or both of the Ctrl or Alt keys, so you might see a shortcut key like this: **Ctrl + Shift + C** (see shortcut p43) which means press all three at the same time.

Keyboard shortcuts help you save time since you never have to take your hands off the keyboard to use the mouse. Incorporating even just a few shortcuts into your daily work is guaranteed to save you time.

Displaying Shortcut Keys

When you hold the mouse pointer over a command button on one of the toolbars, a box will appear naming the command and showing the shortcut key for the command. This is a great way of learning shortcut keys and can help when you are practising. To display Shortcut keys in Windows applications

1. From the **Tools** menu, select **Customize**.

2. In the **Customize** dialog box click the
   Options tab.

3. Under **Other**, select the check boxes:
   Show ScreenTips on toolbars
   and
   Show shortcut keys in ScreenTips.

Note: If you have other components of the Office suite installed on your computer this change will affect all of them.

Function Keys

One of the biggest differences between a typewriter and computer keyboard is the row of keys at the top of the computer keyboard that are labelled F1 through F12 commonly referred to as Function Keys.

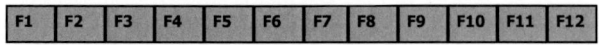

Often overlooked, these function keys provide some interesting shortcuts for common computer functions that can be useful tools in everyday computing. This book will introduce you to the most common default actions of these function keys with MS Windows applications.

The QWERTY Keyboard

The **QWERTY** keyboard takes its name from the first six letters seen in the keyboard's top first row of letters. It is the most common modern-day keyboard layout on English Language computer and typewriter keyboards. Minor variations are made to the arrangement of letters on keyboards for other languages.

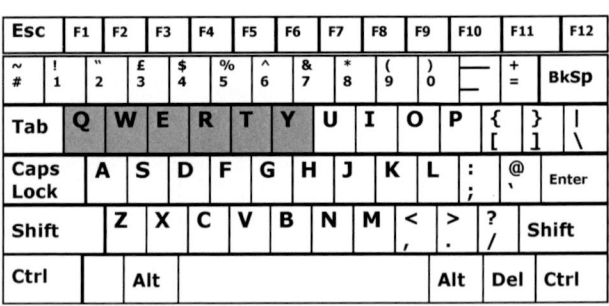

QWERTY is designed for English, a language without any diacritical marks. However, depending on the operating system and sometimes the application program being used there are many ways to generate Latin characters with accents using various key combinations.

Microsoft Office Suite

Microsoft Windows is a series of software operating systems and graphical user interfaces produced by Microsoft. Microsoft first introduced an operating environment named Windows in November 1985 as an add-on to MS-DOS in response to the growing interest in graphical user interfaces. The most recent client version of Windows is Windows Vista.

Microsoft Office is a set of interrelated desktop applications, servers and services, collectively referred to as an office suite, for the Microsoft Windows operating systems.

The desktop applications contained in MS Office include, Word, Excel, Outlook, PowerPoint, and Access being the most common.

The Pocketbook of Shortcut Keys contains the most common shortcuts available for these applications The book also contains shortcut keys for working with Microsoft's graphical web browser : Internet Explorer.

You will find that the shortcut keys for each program work in most versions of the applications including the most recent. However, some keys may be inactive in different versions of the same software application due to upgrades of the software and removal of features.

Accessibility

Today one of the most important issues is that of accessibility for all. Microsoft are continually improving accessibility-related features to the Windows operating system. The Ease of Access Centre in Windows Vista can be used for configuring every aspect of Vista's accessibility features. It allows users to quickly access built-in accessibility tools, like the Magnifier or the Narrator, to explore all settings by category, and to get recommendations for how to use the accessibility options.

For those who have difficulties using a mouse, Windows applications include two other useful options, namely the Keyboard Shortcuts and the Mouse Keys. Keyboard Shortcuts are an application-centric feature, used for many years and not only by those with disabilities.

Every application includes a set of keyboard shortcuts of its own; key combinations which trigger a certain function. The more usual ones, like the ones for saving a file (**Ctrl + S**) or closing a Windows application (**Alt + F4**) are standardized, and common to all Windows applications.

Mouse Keys, also known to those who have used Windows before, allows the mouse cursor to be

Accessibility

manipulated using the arrow keys on the numeric keypad.

For those who can use the keyboard, but not very reliably, Windows Vista offers two options you may be familiar with; Sticky Keys and Filter Keys. Sticky Keys can be used to press sequences of keys, which can be interpreted as key combinations. Instead of pressing Ctrl, Alt and Delete at once, a user can press them in a sequence, and the system will interpret them as a key combination when Sticky Keys is enabled. Filter Keys does the opposite; it ignores keystrokes that occur in rapid succession, or keys which are held down for a longer time than usual.

The 2007 Microsoft Office system is more accessible than ever before, making it easier for everyone to create documents, spreadsheets, and presentations with rich content. The Pocketbook of Shortcut Keys for use with the Microsoft Office Suite of Applications introduces the most useful shortcut keys that can enhance accessibility to many of the major Windows applications. Have fun learning them and increase your productivity by using them.

WORD

Microsoft Word

Microsoft Word is Microsoft's flagship word processing software first released in 1983. Word featured a concept of "What You See Is What You Get", or WYSIWYG, and was the first application with such features as the ability to display bold and italic text on an IBM PC. The latest release is Word 2007 for Windows.

This word processing software package can be used to type letters, reports, and many other documents. The powerful formatting and editing features of Word gives you the ability to use your home computer as well as your business computer for desktop publishing. These features can make your work easier and make your documents more attractive. Word has a built-in spell checker, thesaurus, dictionary and Help facility.

Using shortcut keys to perform many of the most common actions in word processing such as opening a file, cut, copy, or paste text and objects, use the spell checker, use the Find and Replace facility ,change fonts or access the comprehensive Help menu ,will enable you to work more efficiently.

Save time now and start using these amazing shortcut keys whilst working on your Word documents.

1 Save a document

Ctrl + S

Use **Ctrl + S** to save the current file you are working on. This key combination will work in most Windows programs. *The first and most important shortcut key.* Hit these keys periodically and your documents should always be safe.

2 Undo the last operation

Ctrl + Z

Restore your data by undoing any changes quickly and precisely. Use **Ctrl + Z** to quickly undo the last operation performed. Keep pressing to undo multiple changes. This shortcut also works in most Windows applications.

3 Open a document

Ctrl + O

Use **Ctrl + O** to access the Open File Dialogue box and select the document you need to open.

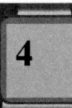

4 Create a new document

Ctrl + N

To create a new document of the same type as the current or most recent document use **Ctrl + N**.

5 Close a document

Ctrl + W

Ctrl + W will close the current document. The Save Changes dialogue box will open if required.

6

Open the Find tab

Ctrl + F

Open the Find dialogue box and search your documents for specific text or data.

7

Open the Replace text tab

Ctrl + H

Open the Replace dialogue box and replace text or data in your document.

8

Open the Go To tab

Ctrl + G

Use **Ctrl + G** to go to a page, footnote, graphic, table or other specific location in your document.

9   Using the Thesaurus

Shift + F7

Use **Shift + F7** to open the Research feature, where you can look up synonyms (different words with the same meaning) and antonyms (words with the opposite meaning) in the thesaurus. See Word shortcut 82 for using the spell-checker facility.

10   Insert a Hyperlink

Ctrl + K

You can *insert a hyperlink* by selecting the item you want to create the link from and using the keyboard shortcut **Ctrl + K** to bring up the "*Hyperlink*" dialogue box where you can specify the link type and target location for the hyperlink.

General Use Keys

11 **Print Layout View**

Alt + Ctrl + P

Switch to Print Layout and see how your document will look when it is printed.

12 **Outline View**

Alt + Ctrl + O

Switch to Outline View to see how your document is organised with outline symbols and indentations.

13 **Normal View**

Alt + Ctrl + N

Switch to Normal View if you are only concerned with entering and editing content.

14 Split a document window

Alt + Ctrl + S

Sometimes you may need to work on two sections of a Word document at the same time. Scrolling back and forth between the two sections is inefficient. Instead, you can split your document window into two horizontal panes using this shortcut.

15 Remove Split window

Alt + Shift + C

When you want to return to a single pane view of your document press **Alt + Shift + C** to remove the split document window setting. Use these two shortcuts to save time alternating between split window settings.

16 **Insert Date Field**

Alt + Shift + D

Insert the date into your document. The default date format can be changed.

17 **Insert Time Field**

Alt + Shift + T

Insert a time field into your document. The default time format can be changed.

18 **Print a Document**

Ctrl + P

Use **Ctrl + P** to open the *Print* dialogue box and select options for printing the current document.

19 Insert a Comment

Alt + Ctrl + M

Inserting comments into a word document is the easiest and most effective way to collaborate and comment on document drafts. Notes inserted using the comments feature can easily be reviewed by scrolling through the document or even hidden, deleted, or printed if one desires.

20 Turn Track Changes On/Off

Ctrl + Shift + E

Track changes is a way for Word to keep track of changes you make to a document. You can choose to display or hide the changes from view. The only way to remove the tracked changes from your document is to accept or reject them.

21 Insert a Footnote

Alt + Ctrl + F

Use footnotes to cite your references. Word automates the process so the numbering is always correct. The footnote mark will appear at the selected location where you use the shortcut and Word will then take you to the footnote section at the bottom of the page.

22 Insert an Endnote

Alt + Ctrl + D

To place a note to a reference, citation, explanation or a comment placed at the end of a work use this shortcut to insert an Endnote. Word automates the process so the numbering is always correct. Numbering formats can be edited.

23   Repeat the last command

Ctrl + Y

Use **Ctrl + Y** to repeat the last command executed. Very handy shortcut key for saving time when you need to repeat an action. For example, if you have formatted text in bold repeat the formatting on a new selection of text by pressing **Ctrl + Y**.

24   Quit Word

Alt + F4

When you're done word processing and don't expect to return to it anytime soon, you can quit (or exit) the Word program using **Alt + F4**. You will be prompted to save any changes to your document before the program closes.

25 **Select a character (R)**

Shift + Right Arrow

Select the character to the right of the insertion point using **Shift + Right Arrow**.

26 **Select a character (L)**

Shift + Left Arrow

Select the character to the left of the cursor using **Shift + Left Arrow**.

27 **Select to end of word**

Ctrl + Shift + Right Arrow

Use this shortcut key to select all the characters from the insertion point to the end of a word.

28

Select to beginning of word

Ctrl + Shift + Left Arrow

Use this shortcut key to select all the characters from the insertion point to the beginning of a word.

29

Select to end of a line

Shift + End

Use **Shift + End** to select all the words from the insertion point to the end of a line of text.

30

Select to beginning of a line

Shift + Home

Use this shortcut key to select all the words from the insertion point to the beginning of a line of text.

31 **Select one line down**

Shift + Down Arrow

Use the **Shift + Down Arrow** key to select the line of text below the insertion point.

32 **Select one line up**

Shift + Up Arrow

Use the **Shift + Up Arrow** key to select the line of text above the insertion point.

33 **Select to end of paragraph**

Ctrl + Shift + Down Arrow

Select all of the text from the insertion point to the end of a paragraph.

34 **Select to end of document**

Ctrl + Shift + End

Select all text and graphics from the insertion point to the end of your document.

35 **Move one screen down**

Shift + Page Down

Use **Shift + Page Down** to move down through your document one screen at a time.

36 **Select an entire document**

Ctrl + A

Select the entire body of a document for quick editing or formatting using **Ctrl + A**.

Keys for Editing Text

37 Cut selected text/objects

Ctrl + X

If you use the Cut Command **Ctrl + X** on any text, objects ,data or files then they disappear from your document and are moved to the clipboard, but are not deleted. Use **Ctrl + V** to paste cut items from the clipboard *(Shortcut Key 39)*.

38 Copy text/objects

Ctrl + C

Select text, objects, or data and use the Copy Command, **Ctrl + C**, to copy the selected items to the clipboard. Increase productivity and use in combination with **Ctrl + V** to paste items from the clipboard *(Shortcut Key 39)*.

39 Paste text/objects

Ctrl + V

In all versions of Word you can paste copied text quickly from the clipboard. Use the paste Command **Ctrl + V** to paste text, objects (pictures etc.), data (tables, charts) from the clipboard to the current cursor position.

40 Move text or graphics

F2; move insertion point + Enter

Move items without using the clipboard. Select the text or image you want to move and press the function key **F2**, move the cursor to where you want to move the item to and then press enter. The text/image will be moved from its current location and inserted at the new insertion point.

41 Insert a field

Ctrl + F3

A field in a Word document is simply a placeholder that contains the instructions for what should go there, such as a date field. Fields will automatically update themselves to reflect information you want to be in the document. Use **Ctrl + F3** to insert a field and right click to edit.

42 Create a screenshot

PrtSc

Pressing the *PrintScreen* key (abbreviated to **PrtSc**) will copy a screenshot of the entire screen as a bitmap image to the clipboard. To copy a screenshot of the currently selected window, *not the entire screen like the normal screenshot function* use **Alt + PrtSc**.

43 Insert © symbol

Alt + Ctrl + C

Use **Ctrl + Alt + C** to insert the **Copyright** symbol © in Word documents.

44 Insert ™ symbol

Alt + Ctrl + T

A **Trademark** ,represented by the symbol ™ can be inserted using the shortcut **Ctrl + Alt + T**.

45 Insert ® symbol

Alt + Ctrl + R

A **Registered Trademark** symbol ® can be inserted using the shortcut **Ctrl + Alt + R**.

46 Insert the € symbol

Alt + Ctrl + E

If your keyboard does not have the Euro € key then use this shortcut to insert the symbol.

47 Insert an ellipsis

Alt + Ctrl + Period

Use this shortcut to insert the most common form of an ellipsis which is a row of three full stops.

48 Insert a page break

Ctrl + Enter

Insert a page break in a Word document where required before the application does it automatically.

49 Cut to the spike

Ctrl + F3

The Spike is an extended Clipboard feature of Microsoft Word. It allows you to remove or cut two or more items (such as text or graphics) from nonadjacent locations in a Word document, and then insert/paste the items as a group in a new location or document *(Shortcut Key 50)*.

50 Paste from the spike

Ctrl + Shift + F3

The items cut to the spike remain in the Spike until you paste them. This shortcut pastes the contents of the spike and empties it at the same time. To add a different set of items to the Spike, you must first empty the Spike's contents. See page 46 for more about the spike's features.

51 Apply bold formatting

Ctrl + B

Turn on **bold** formatting to make text bold as you type or apply **bold** formatting to selected text.

52 Apply underline formatting

Ctrl + U

Turn on <u>underline</u> formatting to underline as you type or apply <u>underline</u> formatting to selected text.

53 Apply italic formatting

Ctrl + I

Turn on *italic* formatting to format text in italics as you type or apply *italic* formatting to selected text.

54 Change the font

Ctrl + Shift + F

Open the font dialogue box to format the font typeface, style, size and effects.

55 Increase font size

Ctrl + Shift + >

Increase the selected font size in a Word document by +2pts for a font size above 12pts.

56 Decrease font size

Ctrl + Shift + <

Decrease the selected font size in a Word document by -2pts for a font size above 12pts.

57 Centre a paragraph

Ctrl + E

Centre text in a document. **Ctrl + E** will centre the selected text to the middle of the page.

58 Justify a paragraph

Ctrl + J

Apply justified text formatting to a document. This will align text with both the left and right margins.

59 Right align a paragraph

Ctrl + R

Right align the text in a document. **Ctrl + R** aligns the selected text to the right of the page.

60 Left align a paragraph

Ctrl + L

Left align the text in a document. **Ctrl + L** aligns the selected text to the left of the page.

61 Indent a paragraph

Ctrl + M

Indent a paragraph in your document. This shortcut will move the paragraph to the first tab point.

62 Create a hanging indent

Ctrl + T

Create a hanging indent in a paragraph. The first line will stick out to the left of the paragraph.

63

Apply a style

Ctrl + Shift + S

Use this shortcut to open the Apply Styles task pane and select a style of your choice.

64

Apply the normal style

Ctrl + Shift + N

Apply the default formatting style to paragraphs in your document. This style can be modified.

65

Apply a list style

Ctrl + Shift + L

Apply the default formatting list style to selected text in your document. This style can be modified.

66

Apply heading style 1

Alt + Ctrl + 1

Apply the default heading style 1 to paragraphs in your document. This style can be modified.

67

Apply heading style 2

Alt + Ctrl + 2

Apply the default heading style 2 to paragraphs in your document. This style can be modified.

68

Apply heading style 3

Alt + Ctrl + 3

Apply the default heading style 3 to paragraphs in your document. This style can be modified.

69 **Apply single line spacing**

Ctrl + 1

Apply single line spacing to a document. This is the default line spacing in Word documents.

70 **Apply double line spacing**

Ctrl + 2

Apply double line spacing to an entire document or a specific section using **Ctrl + 2**.

71 **Apply 1.5 line spacing**

Ctrl + 5

Apply 1.5 line spacing to an entire document or a specific section using **Ctrl + 5**.

72

Apply subscript formatting

Ctrl + Equal sign

Use **Ctrl** + = to apply subscript formatting which makes text smaller and moves it below the baseline. The most common use for subscript text is in chemical formulas. Use subscript formatting to write the formula for acetic acid: $C_2H_4O_2$

73

Apply superscript formatting

Ctrl + Shift + Plus sign

Use **Ctrl** + **Shift** + + to apply superscript formatting which makes text smaller and moves it above the baseline. The most common use for superscript text is maths equations (X^2+1) , footnote numbers[1] and symbols[*] and ordinal numbers (1st) .

41

74 Change case of letter

Shift + F3

Use **Shift** + **F3** to change the text in a Word document from upper to lower case or a capital letter at the beginning of every word. Each time you press this shortcut you will skip through the options for Case changes to your text.

75 Format letters as capitals

Ctrl + Shift + A

Use **Ctrl** + **Shift** + **A** to format all letters as capitals in a Word document. This will convert all text from sentence or lower case to capital letters. To revert back to the previous formatting of a document highlight your selection and press the shortcut again.

76 Review text formatting

Shift + F1

Use **Shift + F1** to open the review formatting pane then slect the text to review its formatting.

77 Copy text formatting

Ctrl + Shift + C

Copy the formatting attributes of text such as font, style, size and colour.

78 Paste text formatting

Ctrl + Shift + V

Paste the formatting attributes of text such as font, style, size and colour to a selection of a document.

79 **Display the help task pane**

F1

Find answers to questions and solutions to problems using Word's Help facility.

80 **Repeat the last command**

F4

Use the **F4** function key to repeat the last command or action (if possible).

81 **Open the Go To tab**

F5

Use the **F5** function key to go to a page, table, graphic or other specific location in your document.

82

Check spelling

F7

Use **F7** to open the spell-check feature in Word to check spelling and grammar in your documents.

83

Select the Menu bar

F10

Use the **F10** function key to activate the menu bar to gain quick access to menu items.

84

Open the Save as dialogue box

F12

Open the Save As dialogue box and save a document with a new name or format using **F12**.

Editing with the Spike

Everyone uses the Clipboard to make edits, but few people know of another powerful way to edit—**using the spike**.

The spike feature allows you to collect groups of text and paste them in another location. It is different than the Clipboard, which allows you to work with only one item at a time. To collect information in the spike, simply select the text and press **Ctrl+F3**. This cuts the information from your document and places it in the Spike. You can continue this process, and Word will add all the selected text to what already exists in the Spike.

When you are ready to paste the information somewhere, simply press **Ctrl+Shift+F3**. All the information in the Spike (*not just the last text you placed there*) is deposited in your document at the insertion point. This action also erases everything in the Spike.

 **Tips to increase productivity**

Quick Tip 1: Use Word's built-in line-generating feature to create a solid line that extends the width of your document. Type three dashes on a new line, and then press Enter and you will get a solid line.

Actually, this works if you enter as few as three dashes, equal signs, or underscores. In each case, Word replaces your characters with a different type of line. **Remember**, to remove the line, you will need to treat it as if you applied a border to a paragraph and remove the border.

The mouse can also be used to increase productivity.

Quick Tip 2: Double click the mouse to select the entire word to the right of the cursor.

Quick Tip 3: Triple click the mouse to select an entire paragraph.

EXCEL

Microsoft Excel

Microsoft Office Excel is a proprietary spreadsheet application written and distributed by Microsoft for Microsoft Windows. It features calculation, graphing tools, pivot tables and also enables users to perform mail merge. Spreadsheets are frequently used for financial information because of their ability to re-calculate an entire worksheet automatically after a change to a single cell is made.

Excel offers many user interface tweaks over the earliest electronic spreadsheets. The Excel program displays cells organized in rows and columns, and each cell contains data or a formula, with relative or absolute references to other cells.

Excel was the first spreadsheet that allowed the user to define the appearance of spreadsheets (fonts, character attributes and cell appearance). It also introduced intelligent cell re-computation, where only cells dependent on the cell being modified are updated. There are many file extension formats available for Excel worksheets but the default Excel file extension format is *.xls*.

For home or office use, Microsoft Office Excel shortcut keys work with all of the current available versions of Excel: Microsoft Excel 97, Excel 2000, Excel 2002, Excel 2003, and Excel 2007 the most current version.

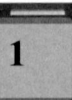

1 Save a spreadsheet file

Ctrl + S

Press **Ctrl + S** periodically while your working to save the current spreadsheet file.

2 Open a spreadsheet

Ctrl + O

Use **Ctrl + O** to access the Open File Dialogue box and select the spreadsheet file you need to open.

3 Create a new spreadsheet

Ctrl + N

To create a new spreadsheet file of the same type as the current or most recent spreadsheet.

4

Close a spreadsheet

Ctrl + W

Ctrl + W will close the current spreadsheet. The Save Changes dialogue box will open if required.

5

Insert a new worksheet

Shift + F11

Use **Shift + F11** to insert a new worksheet at the end of the existing worksheets.

6

Switch between worksheets

Ctrl + Page up/Page Down

Use **Ctrl + Page up/Page Down** to move to the next/ previous worksheet tab in an Excel spreadsheet.

General Use Keys

7 Rename a worksheet

Alt + O,H,R

Use this key sequence to rename a worksheet. The default name will always be 'sheet #'.

8 Delete a worksheet

Alt + E,L

Use this key sequence to delete a worksheet. Excel will ask for confirmation of the delete command.

9 Copy or move a worksheet

Alt + E,M

Use the key sequence **Alt + E, M**, to copy or move a worksheet.

10 View all formulas

Ctrl + ` left apostrophe

To switch between viewing formulas and values on a worksheet press **Ctrl + `** left apostrophe key (grave accent). Pressing the **Ctrl + `** keys again will toggle the formula display off. By enabling the formula display you will not be able to see the calculated values at the same time.

11 Insert a Hyperlink

Ctrl + K

You can *insert a hyperlink* by selecting the item you want to create the link from and using the keyboard shortcut **Ctrl + K** to bring up the "*Hyperlink*" dialogue box where you can specify the link type and target location for the hyperlink.

12 **Open the Find tab**

Ctrl + F

Open the Find dialogue box and search your worksheet for specific data or text.

13 **Open the Replace tab**

Ctrl + H

Open the Replace dialogue box and input the data/ text criteria to find and replace.

14 **Open the Go To tab**

Ctrl + G

Use **Ctrl + G** to go to a specific cell reference, formula , or comment in your worksheet.

15   Print a worksheet

Ctrl + P

Use **Ctrl + P** to open the *Print* dialogue box and select options for printing the current worksheet.

16   Undo the last operation

Ctrl + Z

Use **Ctrl + Z** to quickly undo the last operation performed. Keep pressing to undo multiple changes.

17   Repeat the last command

Ctrl + Y

Use **Ctrl + Y** to repeat the last command executed. An exceptionally useful shortcut when formatting cells.

18 Use the Name Manager

Ctrl + F3

Use the Name Manager dialog box to work with all of the defined names and table names in the workbook. For example, you may want to confirm the value and reference of a name. You can also sort and filter the list of names, and easily add, change, or delete names.

19 Insert a formula

Shift + F3

Select the cell that needs a formula and then use **Shift** + **F3** to open the Insert Function dialog box. When you open the Insert Function dialogue box, Excel automatically selects Most Recently Used as the category and displays the functions you usually use in the Select a Function list box.

20 Create a chart

Alt + F1

Create a chart in Excel with this simple shortcut. Select the data you want to use in the chart and press **Alt + F1**. The chart that is produced uses all the current defaults. If this isn't the type of chart you want to produce you need to change the default chart type.

21 Quit Excel

Alt + F4

Quit Excel using **Alt + F4**. If you haven't already saved the worksheet, you will be asked if you want to save your changes. If you say Yes , you will be asked to give your worksheet a name. Excel will supply the standard filename extension ".xls" by default.

22 Fill down

Ctrl + D

Use the fill down shortcut key to copy data to all the cells selected below the active cell.

23 Fill right

Ctrl + R

Use the fill right shortcut key to copy data to all the cells selected to the right of the active cell.

24 Insert the Euro symbol

Alt + 0128

Use this shortcut key to insert the € symbol. Numbers must be typed on the numeric keypad.

25 Insert an Auto sum

Alt + =

Excel will try to guess what cells you want to total up, either the cells immediately above or to the left.

26 Insert the date

Ctrl + ; (semicolon)

Insert the date into a worksheet. The default date format will be used, but can be changed if required.

27 Insert the time

Ctrl + Shift + :(colon)

Insert the time into a worksheet. The default time format will be used, but can be changed if required.

59

28 **Select an entire column**

Ctrl + Spacebar

Select an entire column including the heading from an active cell anywhere in your worksheet.

29 **Select an entire row**

Shift + Spacebar

Select an entire row from an active cell anywhere in your worksheet using **Shift + Spacebar**.

30 **Select an entire worksheet**

Ctrl + A

Ctrl + A selects the current region. Pressing it a second time selects the entire worksheet.

31

Select cells with comments

Ctrl + Shift + O (the letter O)

Select all cells with comments. Use the tab key to scroll through the selected cells.

32

Cells referenced by formulas

Shift + [(opening bracket)

Use this shortcut key to select cells directly referenced by formulas in the selection.

33

Formulas that reference cells

Shift + [(closing bracket)

Use this shortcut key to select cells that contain formulas that reference the active cell.

34 Cut cells/objects

Ctrl + X

Cut data, text, or objects from your worksheet. Cut items are moved to the clipboard.

35 Copy cells/objects

Ctrl + C

Copy data, text, or objects from your worksheet. Copied items are stored in the clipboard.

36 Paste cells/objects

Ctrl + V

Paste data, text, or objects from the clipboard to an active worksheet or document.

37 Copy formulas

Ctrl + Shift + Left Arrow

Use this shortcut to copy a formula so you can repeat the same formula for many different cells.

38 Paste formulas

Shift + End

Use **Shift + End** to paste formulas to selected cells to repeat the same formulas.

39 Switch between worksheets

Ctrl + Page up/Page Down

Use **Ctrl + Page up/Page Down** to move to the next/ previous worksheet tab in an Excel spreadsheet.

40 **Format cells**

Ctrl + 1

Use **Ctrl + 1** to open the format cells dialogue box to format number, alignment, font and borders etc.

41 **Apply general number format**

Ctrl + Shift + ~

Format a number in general number format. General format cells have no specific number format.

42 **Apply currency format**

Ctrl + Shift + $

Format a number in currency format to two decimal places in the default currency setting.

43 **Apply percentage format**

Ctrl + Shift + %

Apply percentage format to cells so that numbers in the cell are displayed as percentages.

44 **Apply the Number format**

Ctrl + Shift + !

Apply the Number format with two decimal places, thousands separator, or (–) for negative values.

45 **Open the Style dialogue box**

Alt + ' (apostrophe)

Use this shortcut key to review the style formatting for an active cell or selection.

Keys for Formatting Data

46 **Apply bold formatting**

Ctrl + B

Turn on **bold** formatting to make data bold as you type or apply **bold** formatting to selected cell data.

47 **Apply underline formatting**

Ctrl + U

Turn on <u>underline</u> formatting to underline as you type or apply <u>underline</u> formatting to selected data.

48 **Apply italic formatting**

Ctrl + I

Turn on *italic* formatting to format data in italics as you type or apply *italic* formatting to selected data.

49

Apply a strikethrough

Ctrl + 5

Use this shortcut to apply strikethrough formatting to data within a cell. ~~123456~~

50

Apply an outline border

Ctrl + Shift + &

Apply an outline border to a selection of highlighted cells using **Ctrl + Shift + &**.

51

Remove an outline border

Ctrl + Shift + -

Remove an outline border from highlighted cells using **Ctrl + Shift + - (underscore)**.

52 Apply a top border

Alt + T

Working within the border tab in the format cells dialogue box apply or remove a top border.

53 Apply a bottom border

Alt + B

Working within the border tab in the format cells dialogue box apply or remove a bottom border.

54 Apply a left border

Alt + L

Working within the border tab in the format cells dialogue box apply or remove a left border.

55 **Apply a right border**

Alt + R

Working within the border tab in the format cells
dialogue box apply or remove a right border.

56 **Apply a horizontal divider**

Alt + H

Working within the border tab in the format cells
dialogue box apply or remove a horizontal divider.

57 **Apply a vertical divider**

Alt + V

Working within the border tab in the format cells
dialogue box apply or remove a vertical divider.

Keys for Outlining Data

58 Group rows or columns

Alt + Shift + Right Arrow

Use **Alt + Shift + Right Arrow** to group rows or columns of data in your spreadsheet.

59 Ungroup rows or columns

Alt + Shift + Left Arrow

Use **Alt + Shift + Left Arrow** to ungroup rows or columns of data in your spreadsheet.

60 Hide rows

Ctrl + 9

Use **Ctrl + 9** to hide rows of information or data in your spreadsheet without affecting calculations.

61

Unhide rows

Ctrl + Shift + (

Use **Ctrl + Shift + (** (opening parenthesis) to **un**hide rows of data in your spreadsheet.

62

Hide columns

Ctrl + 0 (zero)

Use **Ctrl + 0** (zero) to hide columns data in your spreadsheet without affecting calculations.

63

Unhide columns

Ctrl + Shift +)

Use **Ctrl + Shift +)** (closing parenthesis) to **un**hide columns of data in your spreadsheet .

64

Display Help task pane

F1

Find answers to questions and solutions to problems using Excel's Help facility using **F1**.

65

Edit the active cell

F2

Use **F2** to edit the active cell and position the insertion point at the end of the cell contents.

66

Repeat the last action

F4

Use the **F4** function key to repeat the last command or action (if possible).

67 Display the Go To dialogue box

F5

Use the **F5** function key to go to a specific cell reference in your worksheet.

68 Create a chart

F11

Select the data you want to use in the chart and press **F11** to produce a chart with the default settings.

69 Open the Save As dialogue box

F12

Open the Save As dialogue box and save a spreadsheet with a new name or format using **F12**.

The Fill Handle

Possibly one of Excels most under utilized features is the **Fill Handle** ; the small black square in the bottom right of the active cell. In it's simplest form it will increment any series of numbers. For example, if you type the number 1 in any cell and then the number 2 in a cell that adjoins it, you can use the Fill Handle to increment up to any number desired. To do this you simply select your two cells and then hover your mouse pointer over the Fill Handle (until it changes to a small black cross), left click and drag in the direction you want the incremented numbers to show.

You can also do the same by entering any starting number in any cell, selecting the cell, holding down the **Ctrl** key and then dragging down with the Fill Handle. If you do not hold down the **Ctrl** key Excel will simply copy the same number. The exact same principle applies to dates.

Viewing Hidden Top Rows

Excel makes it easy to hide and unhide rows using shortcut keys. What isn't so easy is displaying a hidden row if that row is above the first visible row in the worksheet. For instance, if you hide rows 1 through 5, Excel will dutifully follow out your instructions. If you later want to unhide any of these rows, the solution isn't so obvious. To unhide the top rows of a worksheet when they are hidden, follow these steps:

- Press **F5**. Excel displays the Go To dialog box.
- In the Reference field at the bottom of the dialogue box, enter the number of the row range that you want to unhide. For instance, if you want to unhide rows 1 through 3, enter **1:3**.
- Click on OK. The rows you specified are now selected, even though you cannot see it on the screen.

Use the shortcut **Ctrl + Shift + (** to unhide rows and the selected rows will now be visible again.

ACCESS

Microsoft Access

Microsoft Office Access, is a relational database management system that is generally used by small businesses, within departments of large corporations, and by hobby programmers to create *ad hoc* customized desktop systems for handling the creation and manipulation of data.

Access allows relatively quick development because of very good graphic user interface design tools that do not require deep database development knowledge to create effective databases. Use Access to create database tables for storing data records in columns and rows, queries for retrieving information from the database, forms for inputting and displaying information, and reports that display sorted, filtered, and grouped information in a way that helps you make sense of the data for informed decision-making. All these database objects are stored in the database. Access also allows users to also collect information by importing data from external applications such as Excel spreadsheets or Outlook express contact records.

The current Access 2007 file format (.accdb) is different from previous versions of Access (.mdb), however databases with the .mdb format can be easily converted to the new file format. Increase your keyboard productivity with this range of Access shortcut keys.

1 Save a database object

Ctrl + S

Press **Ctrl + S** periodically while your working to save the current database object.

2 Open an existing database

Ctrl + O

Use **Ctrl + O** to display the Open File Dialogue box and open an existing database file.

3 Create a new database

Ctrl + N

Create a new database file of the same type as the current or most recent database.

4

Open the Find tab

Ctrl + F

Open the Find tab in the Find and Replace dialogue box (Datasheet view and Form view only).

5

Open the Replace tab

Ctrl + H

Open the Replace tab in the Find and Replace dialogue box (Datasheet view and Form view only).

6

Repeat find action

Shift + F4

Repeat the find action when the Find and Replace dialogue box is closed.

7 **Cut data/objects**

Ctrl + X

Cut data, text, or objects from your database. Cut items are moved to the clipboard.

8 **Copy data/objects**

Ctrl + C

Copy data, text, or objects from your database. Copied items are stored in the clipboard.

9 **Paste data/objects**

Ctrl + V

Paste data, text, or objects from the clipboard to an active object in your database.

10

Print a database object

Ctrl + P

Use **Ctrl + P** to open the *Print* dialogue box and print the current selection or object.

11

Undo the last operation

Ctrl + Z

Use **Ctrl + Z** to quickly undo the last operation performed. Keep pressing to undo multiple changes.

12

Open a property sheet

Alt + V, P

Use **Alt + V,P** to open a property sheet for a selected object and change its attributes/characteristics.

13 Expand a subdatasheet

Ctrl + Shift + Down Arrow

To expand a subdatasheet for a row of a datasheet or subdatasheet use **Ctrl + Shift + Down Arrow**.

14 Collapse a subdatasheet

Ctrl + Shift + Up Arrow

To collapse a subdatasheet for a row of a datasheet or subdatasheet use **Ctrl + Shift + Up Arrow**.

15 Exit a subdatasheet

Ctrl + Tab

Exit the subdatasheet and move to the first field of the next record in the datasheet.

16

Add a control

Shift + Enter

Add a control to a section using **Shift + Enter**, choose the control type as label, box or button.

17

Move a control right

Ctrl + Right Arrow

Reposition a control. Move the selected control to the right by a pixel (irrespective of the page's grid).

18

Move a control left

Ctrl + Left Arrow

Reposition a control. Move the selected control to the left by a pixel (irrespective of the page's grid).

19 Move a control up

Ctrl + Up Arrow

Reposition a control. Move the selected control up by a pixel (irrespective of the page's grid).

20 Move a control down

Ctrl + Down Arrow

Reposition a control. Move the selected control down by a pixel (irrespective of the page's grid).

21 Increase a control width

Shift + Right Arrow

Resize a control. Increase the width of the selected control (to the right) by a pixel.

22 **Decrease a control width**

Shift + Left Arrow

Resize a control. Decrease the width of the selected control (to the left) by a pixel.

23 **Increase a control height**

Shift + Down Arrow

Resize a control. Increase the height of the selected control (from the bottom) by a pixel.

24 **Decrease a control height**

Shift + Up Arrow

Resize a control. Decrease the height of the selected control (from the bottom) by a pixel.

25 View next wizard window

Alt + N

To move to the next window in the wizard as you create new objects or perform actions use **Alt + N**.

26 View previous wizard window

Alt + B

Move back to the previous window in the wizard as you create new objects or perform actions.

27 Close the wizard window

Alt + F

Use **Alt + F** to close the wizard window. You will be prompted to ensure you want to close the wizard.

28 Switch views

Shift + F7

The Visual Basic Editor, included with most Office programs is the environment you use to create, modify, and manage access macros. To switch views from the Visual Basic Editor to form or report design view use the shortcut key **Shift + F7**.

29 Quit Access

Alt + F4

Quit Access using **Alt + F4**. If you haven't already saved the database, you will be asked if you want to save your changes. If you say Yes , you will be asked to give your document a name. Access 2007 will supply the standard filename extension ".accdb" by default.

30 Select all records

Ctrl + A

Press **Ctrl + A** to select all records in a database table for editing or formatting.

31 Select next record

Shift + Down Arrow

Use **Shift + Down Arrow** to select the next record in your database table.

32 Select current column

Ctrl + Spacebar

Use **Ctrl + Spacebar** to select the current column in a table. Also used to cancel a column selection.

33

Select right column

Shift + Right Arrow

To select the column to the right, if the current column in a table is selected.

34

Select left column

Shift + Left Arrow

To select the column to the left, if the current column in a table is selected.

35

Move columns left or right

Ctrl + Shift + F8

Turn on Move mode and use the arrow keys to move selected column (s); press **Esc** when finished.

36 Insert the date

Ctrl + ; (semi colon)

Insert the current date into a record. The default date format will be used.

37 Insert the time

Ctrl + Shift + : (colon)

Insert the current time into a table field. The default time format will be used.

38 Add a new record

Ctrl + + (plus sign)

Add a new record to a database table using the shortcut **Ctrl + +**.

39

Delete a current record

Ctrl + - (minus sign)

Select a record in a table and delete it using the shortcut **Ctrl + -** .

40

Save changes to a record

Shift + Enter

Save changes to a current record in a table.

41

Insert a default value

Ctrl + Alt + Spacebar

Insert the default value into a field using the shortcut **Ctrl + Alt + Spacebar**.

42 **Cycle through the objects bar**

Ctrl + Tab

Cycle through the objects bar (Access navigation menu) from top to bottom using **Ctrl + Tab**.

43 **Cycle through the objects bar**

Shift + Ctrl + Tab

Use **Shift + Ctrl + Tab** to cycle through the objects bar from bottom to top.

44 **Open a Table or Query**

Alt + O

This shortcut will open the objects window where a table or query can be selected and opened.

45 **Open object in design view**

Alt + D

Make changes to Access objects (tables, queries, reports etc.) by opening them in design view.

46 **Create a new object**

Alt + N

Create a new Access object (table, query, report etc.) using the shortcut **Alt + N**.

47 **Display the immediate window**

Ctrl + G

Display the immediate window to view or test your code using the shortcut **Ctrl + G**.

48 Display Help task pane

F1

Find answers to questions and solutions to problems using Access' Help facility.

49 Go to a specific record

F5

Go to a specific record by pressing **F5**, type the record number in the dialogue box and press enter.

50 Switch between views

F6

Switch between the help task pane and the program window with the **F6** function key.

51

Select the menu bar

F10

Use the **F10** function key to Activate the menu bar to gain quick access to menu items.

52

View the database window

F11

Bring the database window to the front with the **F11** function key.

53

Open the Save As dialogue box

F12

Open the Save As dialogue box and save a database with a new name or format using **F12**.

Adding custom shortcut keys

Custom shortcut keys can make navigating through your database far easier. If you want to be able to quickly switch to a particular field on a form you can do so with a shortcut key.

To assign a shortcut key to a field, edit the caption property of the label of the particular control you want to jump to, adding an **'&'** before the letter you want to act as the shortcut key.

For example, if you wish to be able to jump to a 'Name' field you could edit the 'Name' label accordingly:

N&ame

In Form View the label will be displayed with the 'a' in name underlined:

N<u>a</u>me

Pressing **Alt-A** will switch the focus to the 'Name' field. This technique can be used on any object that has a caption property.

Tips to increase productivity

Quick Tip 1: Copy a previous record's values into a new record and save re-typing the same data. Use the shortcut **Ctrl + '** (apostrophe) to repeat the value input in the previous record.

Quick Tip 2: Hide the rows and columns in tables by reducing their height and width. You can reduce the width of a column in table by using the mouse to drag the column edge to the desired width. Position your mouse pointer at the right of the field selector for that column and drag it to the left. If you drag it beyond the left hand side of the column you will hide the column.

You can decrease the height of a row in a table in a similar way. Simply position the mouse between the two record selectors at the left side of the table and drag to the required height. When you change the height of the row it will make all rows for that table the same. For this reason you cannot hide the row by dragging the bottom above the top of the row as it would hide all rows for the table.

OUTLOOK

Outlook

Microsoft Office Outlook is a powerful personal information manager and is part of the Microsoft Office Suite (current version MS Outlook 2007). Outlook is mainly used as an e-mail application, which means you can use it to send and receive e-mail, store information about your contacts, including their e-mail addresses, then use Outlook to keep in touch with them via e-mail.

Outlook also includes an appointment calendar, forms for entering information about appointments, contacts, and tasks, a journal, and electronic sticky notes. Outlook is used to keep track of your appointments and meetings, manage your business and personal contacts, maintain a to-do list, and keep a record of your activities (files you work on, phone calls you make).

Outlook can be used as a stand-alone application, but can also operate in conjunction with Microsoft Exchange Server and Microsoft Office SharePoint Server to provide enhanced functions for multiple users in an organization, such as shared mailboxes and calendars, Exchange public folders, Sharepoint lists and meeting time allocation.

Use this selection of shortcut keys for Outlook and increase your productivity whilst using this personal information manager application.

1   Create an Appointment

Ctrl + Shift + A

Create a new appointment with location, subject and time.

2   Create a Contact

Ctrl + Shift + C

Create a new contact and add it to your address book.

3   Create a Distribution list

Ctrl + Shift + L

Create a new distribution list (group of contacts) that is stored by default in the Contacts folder.

4

Create a Fax

Ctrl + Shift + X

Use **Ctrl + Shift + X** to create and send a fax to recipients using Outlook.

5

Create a Journal Entry

Ctrl + Shift + J

Create a journal entry related to contacts for messages, meeting and task requests and responses.

6

Create a Meeting request

Ctrl + Shift + Q

Create a meeting request with attendees, time, location and subject using **Ctrl + Shift + Q**.

7

Create a Message

Ctrl + Shift + M

Use **Ctrl + Shift + M** to open the new message form wherever you are in Outlook.

8

Create a Note

Ctrl + Shift + N

The fastest way to create a note regardless of where you are in Outlook is to use **Ctrl + Shift +N**.

9

Create a Task

Ctrl + Shift + K

Open the Task window and use the Task and Details tabs to record the task name and details.

10

Forward an item

Ctrl + F

Use **Ctrl + F** to forward a message, appointment, meeting request ,task or note.

11

Jump to a different folder

Ctrl + Y

Outlook will normally open with a default folder. Use **Ctrl + Y** to jump quickly to a different folder.

12

Print current document

Ctrl + P

Use **Ctrl + P** to open the Print dialogue box and print the current document.

General Use Keys

13 To switch to Mail

Ctrl + 1

Use **Ctrl + 1** to switch to Mail view. The Mail view will open with the default view.

14 To switch to Calendar

Ctrl + 2

Switch to Calendar view using **Ctrl + 2**. The calendar will be displayed with the default view.

15 To switch to Contacts

Ctrl + 3

View all your contact information. Switch to Contacts view using **Ctrl + 3**.

16 **To switch to Tasks**

Ctrl + 4

Switch to Tasks view using **Ctrl + 4** to view all your **'To do'** lists. This view can be customised.

17 **To switch to Notes**

Ctrl + 5

Switch to Notes view using **Ctrl + 5** to view all your Notes . This view can be customised.

18 **To switch to Folder list**

Ctrl + 6

View all of your Outlook folders by switching to Folder view using **Ctrl + 6**.

19 To switch to Inbox

Ctrl + Shift + I

View all incoming mail. Switch to the Inbox folder in Outlook using the shortcut **Ctrl + Shift + I**.

20 To switch to Outbox

Ctrl + Shift + O

View all mail in the Outbox. Switch to the Outbox folder using the shortcut **Ctrl + Shift + O**.

21 Check for new mail

Ctrl + M

Use **Ctrl + M** to check your sever for new mail. The 'Check for new mail' setting can be customised.

22

Compose a message

Ctrl + N

Use **Ctrl + N** to open a new message form and add recipients, subject and the body of the message.

23

Display the Address Book

Ctrl + Shift + B

Open and display the Address book dialogue box to select , amend, or edit a contacts list.

24

Send a message

Alt + S

When an email has been composed and is ready to send use **Alt + S** to send the email.

25 Open a message

Ctrl + O

Open a selected message for viewing, printing or forwarding using the shortcut **Ctrl + O**.

26 Reply to a message

Ctrl + R

This shortcut will open a new message form and automatically insert the recipients address.

27 Post message to a folder

Ctrl + Shift + S

Use this shortcut to post a message to a folder. Select the email and post it to a destination folder.

28

Mark message as read

Ctrl + Q

Use **Ctrl + Q** to manually mark a message as read. Outlook can be set to do this automatically.

29

Mark message as unread

Ctrl + U

Use **Ctrl + U** to manually mark a message as unread. Outlook can be set to do this automatically.

30

Mark message as not junk

Ctrl + Alt + J

Mark a message as not junk. Outlook will prompt you to add sender to safe sender/recipient list.

31

Display Help task pane

F1

Find answers to questions and solutions to problems using Outlook's Help facility.

32

Display the Find bar

F3

Pressing **F3** will display the Find tab to search for a message or item using search criteria.

33

Switch between views

F6

Switch between views in Outlook using the Function key **F6**.

34 Check Spelling

F7

Avoid spelling mistakes and use **F7** to check spelling in an email message before you send it.

35 Check for new mail

F9

Use **F9** to check your sever for new mail. The 'Check for new mail' setting can be customised .

36 Save a message

F12

Open the Save As dialogue box and save a message with a new name or format using **F12**.

Vote by Email

Need to ask a group of people where to eat for lunch, or whether they approve or disapprove of a policy change or anything else that requires a vote? Well you can by adding voting options to your email when sending email to other Outlook users.

To do so:

1. When composing an e-mail message, click the "Options" button.

2. When the "Message Options" dialog box appears, click "Use voting buttons".

3. Click on the pull-down next to the button to choose the voting options such as "Yes;No", or enter your own questions, separated by a semicolon.

4. Click the "Close" dialog box.

5. Continue to compose and send your message.

Voting buttons work in all versions of Outlook.

Reviewing Voting Responses

When your message is received, recipients will have the option to vote on the e-mail by clicking on voting buttons or a message Infobar. Responses will be sent to your Inbox as e-mail messages.

To view the official tally:

1. Click on your "Sent Items" folder.

2. Open the original e-mail in a new window (double-click the e-mail).

You will now see who received your message, and Outlook maintains a running total of responses at the top of the Tracking tab on the sent message.

Note that people can change their vote at any time, and you will need to close and re-open the original mail to see the current tally.

After you send a voting-button message, don't move it from your Sent Items folder. If you move the message to another folder, Outlook won't be able to process the responses.

POWERPOINT

PowerPoint

Microsoft PowerPoint is the presentation graphics component of the Office suite. Use PowerPoint to create effective, attractive slide presentations you can project on screen through the computer. You can also create handouts for your audience and notes for yourself.

Getting started with PowerPoint is easy. PowerPoint has many features to help you to convey your message effectively. There are Wizards to guide you through creating common presentations, presentation templates that provide ready-made models to get you started, and design templates to give your presentations a polished, professional look.

Use PowerPoint alone, or tap into the real power of Microsoft Office by using it with the other applications in the suite. For example you can outline your ideas in Word, then open your Word document in PowerPoint and watch PowerPoint create a slide for each heading in the outline; Create graphs in Excel, then paste them into PowerPoint. You can save your presentations as self-running shows or Web pages.

Practicing and using PowerPoint shortcut keys is an effective way of increasing productivity and performance when creating or delivering presentations.

1 Save a Presentation file

Ctrl + S

Press **Ctrl + S** periodically while your working to save the current PowerPoint file.

2 Open a Presentation File

Ctrl + O

Use **Ctrl + O** to access the Open File Dialogue box and select the presentation file you need to open.

3 Create a new presentation

Ctrl + N

Use **Ctrl + N** to create a new presentation file of the same type as the current presentation file.

4 **Close a presentation file**

Ctrl + W

Ctrl + W will close the current presentation. The Save Changes dialogue box will open if required.

5 **Minimize a window**

Ctrl + F9

Reduce clutter on your desktop using the shortcut **Ctrl + F9** to minimize a window to an icon.

6 **Maximize a window**

Ctrl + F10

Open a window to the maximum size of the desktop display area using **Ctrl + F10**.

7 Show/Hide grid lines

Shift + F9

Show or Hide the gridlines used to identify the center of a slide and position shapes and objects.

8 Show/Hide guide lines

Alt + F9

Show or Hide the drawing guidelines used to position shapes and objects on a slide.

9 Change grid/guide settings

Ctrl + G

Change the grid or guide lines setting by choosing from a range of preset measurements.

Group Objects

Ctrl + Shift + G

Grouping objects in PowerPoint makes them easier to manipulate as the grouped objects behaves as if they were one object. To group AutoShape, picture, or WordArt objects, select the items you want to group by holding down the Shift key and then press **Ctrl + Shift + G**.

Ungroup Objects

Ctrl + Shift + H

To ungroup a group, select the group, and then press **Ctrl + Shift + H**. After you have ungrouped objects you don't have to reselect them all again to *regroup* the objects using the Shift and click method, simply use the *regroup* shortcut key **Ctrl + Shift + J** to regroup all objects again.

12 Undo the last operation

Ctrl + Z

Use **Ctrl + Z** to quickly undo the last operation performed. Keep pressing to undo multiple changes.

13 Repeat the last command

Ctrl + Y

Use **Ctrl + Y** to repeat the last command executed, excellent key when formatting or editing.

14 Print a Presentation

Ctrl + P

Use **Ctrl + P** to open the *Print* dialogue box and select options for printing the current presentation.

15   Insert a Hyperlink

Ctrl + K

You can *insert a hyperlink* by selecting the item you want to create the link from and using the keyboard shortcut **Ctrl + K** to bring up the "*Hyperlink*" dialogue box where you can specify the link type and target location for the hyperlink.

16   Quit PowerPoint

Alt + F4

Quit PowerPoint using **Alt + F4**. If you haven't already saved the presentation, you will be asked if you want to save your changes. If you say Yes , you will be asked to give your document a name. PowerPoint will supply the standard filename extension ".pps" (2007 version) by default.

17 Stop/Start a Slideshow

S

Stop and restart a slideshow presentation simply using the shortcut (letter) **S** on a keyboard.

18 Go To a slide

number + **Enter**

Type the number of the slide you wish to go to and press **Enter**.

19 Advance to next slide

N

Advance to the next slide. Works even if all objects have not been displayed on the current slide.

20

Return to previous slide

P

Return to the previous slide. Works even if all objects have not been displayed on the current slide.

21

Display a black screen

B

To display a black screen during a presentation or return to the slideshow from a black screen.

22

Display a white screen

W

To display a white screen during a presentation or return to the slideshow from a white screen.

Working with presentations

123

23 **Change pointer to a pen**

Ctrl + P

Change the pointer to a pen during a presentation using the shortcut **Ctrl + P**.

24 **Change pointer to an arrow**

Ctrl + A

Use the shortcut **Ctrl + A** to change the pointer to an arrow during a presentation.

25 **Hide the pointer**

Ctrl + H

Keep distractions to a minimum during a slideshow and hide the pointer using **Ctrl + H**.

Working with presentations

26 Erase onscreen annotations

E

Use the shortcut **E** to erase annotations created on your slide using the annotation pen.

27 Return to first slide

1 + Enter

Return to the first slide in a slideshow using the shortcut **1 + Enter**.

28 End a slide show

Esc

Use the **Esc** key to exit a slideshow at any time and return to Normal view (default view in PowerPoint).

29

Cut selected object

Ctrl + X

Cut data, text, or objects from your presentation. Cut items are moved to the clipboard.

30

Copy selected object

Ctrl + C

Copy data, text, or objects from your presentation. Copied items are stored in the clipboard.

31

Paste selected object

Ctrl + V

Paste data, text, or objects from the clipboard to an active presentation.

32 Select all objects/slides/text

Ctrl + A

Select all objects on the slides tab, all slides in slide sorter view, or all text on the outline tab.

33 Insert a slide

Ctrl + M

Insert a new blank/template slide at the current position in your slide show using **Ctrl + M**.

34 Duplicate a slide

Ctrl + D

Duplicate a selected slide using **Ctrl + D**, the slide can then be pasted anywhere in a presentation.

35 **Apply bold formatting**

Ctrl + B

Turn on **bold** formatting to make text bold as you type or apply **bold** formatting to selected text.

36 **Apply underline formatting**

Ctrl + U

Turn on <u>underline</u> formatting to underline as you type or apply <u>underline</u> formatting to selected text.

37 **Apply italic formatting**

Ctrl + I

Turn on *italic* formatting to format text in italics as you type or apply *italic* formatting to selected text.

38

Change the font

Ctrl + Shift + F

Open the font dialogue box to format font typeface, style, size and effects.

39

Increase font size

Ctrl + Shift + >

Increase the selected font size by +2pts for a font size above 12pts.

40

Decrease font size

Ctrl + Shift + <

Decrease the selected font size by -2pts for a font size above 12pts.

Formatting Presentations

129

41

Centre a paragraph

Ctrl + E

Centre text in a text box. **Ctrl + E** will centre the selected text to the middle of a text box/object.

42

Justify a paragraph

Ctrl + J

Apply justified text formatting which aligns text with both the left and right margins of a text box/object.

43

Right align a paragraph

Ctrl + R

Right align text in a paragraph. **Ctrl + R** aligns the selected text to the right of a text box/object.

44

Apply subscript formatting

Ctrl + Equal sign

Use **Ctrl** + = to apply subscript formatting which makes text smaller and moves it below the baseline. The most common use for subscript text is in chemical formulas. Use subscript formatting to write the formula for acetic acid: $C_2H_4O_2$

45

Apply superscript formatting

Ctrl + Shift + Plus sign

Use **Ctrl** + **Shift** + + to apply superscript formatting which makes text smaller and moves it above the baseline. The most common use for superscript text is maths equations (X^2+1), footnote numbers[1] and symbols[*] and ordinal numbers (1st).

46 Change case of letter

Shift + F3

Use **Shift + F3** to change text in a text box/object from upper to lower case or a capital letter at the beginning of every word. Each time you press this shortcut you will skip through the options for Case changes to your text.

47 Format letters as capitals

Ctrl + Shift + A

Use **Ctrl + Shift + A** to format all letters as capitals in a text box/object. This will convert all text from sentence or lower case to capital letters. To revert back to the previous formatting of a document highlight your selection and press the shortcut again.

48

Remove formatting

Ctrl + Spacebar

Remove manual character formatting such as subscript and superscript.

49

Copy text formatting

Ctrl + Shift + C

Copy the formatting attributes of text such as font, style, size and colour.

50

Paste text formatting

Ctrl + Shift + V

Paste the formatting attributes of text such as font, style, size and colour to a section of a slideshow.

53 **Display Help task pane**

F1

Find answers to questions and solutions to problems using PowerPoint's Help facility.

 54 **Repeat the last action**

F4

Use the **F4** function key to repeat the last command or action (if possible).

 55 **Begin a Slide show**

F5

Begin a slide show. Press **F5** and PowerPoint will display the first slide of (or run) the slideshow.

56 Switch between views

F6

Switch between views in PowerPoint using the Function key **F6**.

57 Check Spelling

F7

Use **F7** to open the spell-check feature in PowerPoint to check spelling and grammar.

58 Save a Slide show

F12

Open the Save As dialogue box and save a Slide Show with a new name or format using **F12**.

Animate Individual Pie Slices

Although you can animate pie charts using the **Chart Effects** feature in the **Custom Animation** dialog box, you can also animate individual pie slices.

Click your pie chart and select **Ungroup** from the **Draw** menu (**Drawing** toolbar). Click **Yes** to confirm. This splits each pie slice into several pieces. Now select all the pieces that go to make up a single pie slice:

- Click one piece to select it.
- Hold down the **Shift** key and click the other pieces one by one.
- Select **Group** from the **Draw** menu to make a group of this one slice. Repeat for each of the other slices.

Once all the slices are grouped, you can set the options on the **Order and Timing** tab and the **Effects** tab of the **Custom Animation** dialog box to animate your chart. Now that each pie slice is its own group, you can choose the order in which the slices will appear, as well as the effect for each slice.

 **Linking and Embedding files**

There may be times when you want to include information (tables, charts etc.) or Audio and video files in a Microsoft Office PowerPoint presentation. To do this you can either embed or link the objects to your presentation.

Embedded files are stored within the presentation, and linked files are stored outside the presentation. The difference between embedded and liked files is that linked files are updated when changes are made to the source file (a connection is maintained to the source file), but embedded files don't change if the source file is changed.

When your presentation contains linked files, you must copy both the linked files and the presentation if you plan to give the presentation on another computer or send it to someone in an e-mail message. Copying the files into the same folder as the presentation makes the files available to Microsoft Office PowerPoint 2007, so that PowerPoint can find the files when you want to run them.

INTERNET
EXPLORER

Internet Explorer

Internet Explorer (formerly Microsoft Internet Explorer), commonly abbreviated to **IE**, is a series of graphical web browsers developed by Microsoft. The adoption rate of Internet Explorer seems to be closely related to that of Microsoft Windows, as it is the default web browser that comes with Windows. It is the most widely used web browser with currently about 90% usage share. The most recent release is version Internet Explorer 7.

Internet Explorer has been designed to view a broad range of web pages and to provide certain features within the operating system, including:

- Tabbed browsing; View multiple sites in a single browser window
- Quick Tabs; Easily select and navigate through open tabs by displaying thumbnails of them all in a single window
- Advanced printing options
- Favorites center giving quick access to your favorites web pages
- Page zooming for more accessibility

You can use shortcut keys with **IE** to view and explore Web pages, preview pages before you print, use the Address box, work with favorites, and edit.

1

Return to home page

Alt + Home

Return to the home page, the web page that appears when you start Internet Explorer.

2

Open a new window

Ctrl + N

Use **Ctrl + N** to open a new browser window. There will now be two windows open at the same time.

3

Quick address entry

Ctrl + Enter

Add **"www."** to the beginning and **".com"** to the end of the text that you type in the Address box.

4 **Display Help task pane**

F1

Find answers to questions and solutions to problems using Internet Explorer's Help facility.

5 **Stop downloading a page**

Esc

Stop a page downloading or terminate a long directory search using the **Esc** key.

6 **Open a link in a new window**

Shift

Hold down the **Shift** key while clicking a hyperlink to open the link in a new window.

7 Open the Favorites Menu

Alt + A

Open the Favorites menu bar and navigate to a web page, or organise your favorite web pages.

8 Add a page to Favorites

Ctrl + D

Use **Ctrl + D** to add any web page you visit frequently to your favorites folder.

9 Organize Favorites Folder

Ctrl + B

Open the organise favourites menu where you can move, rename or delete your favorite web pages.

10 Open Favorites Menu Box

Ctrl + I

Ctrl + I will open the Favorites menu box where you can add, organise or go to a favourite web.

11 Open History Box

Ctrl + H

View visited websites of Internet Explorer using **Ctrl + H**. History settings can be modified.

12 Display Address list

F4

Use the function key F4 to display a list of addresses you have typed or visited.

13 **Select all objects on a page**

Ctrl + A

Select all objects and text on a web page to print or copy and paste to another application.

14 **Highlight the address bar**

Alt + D

Use **Alt + D** to highlight the text in the address bar which can then be edited or deleted and replaced.

15 **Refresh a page**

F5

Keep web page content up to date and refresh your web page with a fresh copy from the server.

16 Open Print dialogue box

Ctrl + P

Use **Ctrl + P** to open the *Print* dialogue box and select options for printing the current web page.

17 Toggle between views

F11

Use **F11** to toggle between full screen and other views in the browser.

18 Close Browser window

Ctrl + W

Close the current browser window using the shortcut **Ctrl + W**.

 **Changing text size**

Having trouble reading certain web pages in Internet Explorer 7 as the text size is too small? Or do you want to cram more information on a page without having to scroll? Here are two options to change the text size on web pages:

If you have a "Wheel" mouse:

- Hold down the Ctrl key while moving the wheel down to decrease the text size. Hold down the Ctrl key while moving the wheel up to increase the text size.

Via the keyboard:

- Ctrl + 0 to reset the zoom size to default(100%)
- Ctrl + + to increase the text size
- Ctrl + - to decrease the text size

NOTE: Internet Explorer 7 may get confused if you use both methods of changing zoom levels. Use Ctrl + 0 to reset the text size to the default if this problem occurs.

Send a web page link

Found an entertaining, informative, or useful website while browsing the web with Internet Explorer and wish to share it with your friends, family, or officemates? If you use client-based e-mail software such as Outlook 2003 or Outlook Express, Internet Explorer makes this easy.

- Click the "Page" button, selecting "Send Link by E-Mail".
- Your default e-mail program will open. The message subject will contain the title of the currently-browsed webpage, and the body will contain a hyperlink to that webpage
- Enter your recipient, edit the message body, subject, or other fields as needed, and send away

Quick tip:Clear History Folder

By default, Internet Explorer keeps tracks of the most-recent websites you have visited through a website history function. To clear the items listed in the history click on the "Tools" menu, and select "Delete Browsing History".

WINDOWS
KEY

Windows Key

The Windows key or Windows logo key (in short WinKey), is a keyboard key originally introduced for the Windows 95 operating system. Microsoft regulates the appearance of the Windows key with a specially crafted license for keyboard manufacturers. Normally, a Windows key is placed between the left control key and the left alt key; In laptop and other compact keyboards it is also common to have a Windows key (usually on the left).

The Windows key can also generally be used under different operating systems. Under Unix and Unix-like operating systems it is often used as the Meta key or Compose key. On keyboards lacking a Windows key, **Ctrl + Esc** can instead be pressed, though some functionality may be lacking.

Pressing the Windows key in combination with other keys performs many common functions through the keyboard. What Windows key combinations ("shortcuts") are available and active in a given Windows session depends on many factors, including accessibility options, the Windows version and the presence of specific software.

Increase your productivity using these Windows Key Shortcuts to complete some of the most common everyday computer tasks, you will be amazed at how much easier and faster you can work.

Introduction

1 Open the Start menu

 Windows Key

Open the Start menu to launch applications and tasks using the **Windows key**.

2 Display the Desktop

 Windows Key + D

Use the **Windows key + D** to minimise all windows and show the desktop. Depress again to resume.

3 Open Explorer window

 Windows Key + E

Opens a new Explorer Window. Probably one of the hottest Windows keyboard shortcuts.

4 **Open Search dialogue box**

 Windows Key + F

Use the **Windows key + F** to open the Search dialogue box for files and folders.

5 **Lock the Desktop**

 Windows Key + L

For added security lock your computer instantly using the **Windows key + L**.

6 **Switch between open items**

 Windows Key + Tab

Keeping the **Windows key** depressed, press the **Tab key** to switch between all open items.

Function (FN) Keys

The **FN**, or 'Function,' key is a modifier key on many keyboards used in a compact layout to combine keys which are usually kept separate. It is typically found on laptops, since a full sized keyboard would be difficult to fit in a laptop chassis. It is also found in many full-sized 'multimedia' and 'office' keyboards, named F Lock key. It is mainly for the purpose of changing display or audio settings quickly, and is held down in conjunction with the appropriate key to change the settings. These keys are usually marked by special icons, and these icons are color coded to match the **FN** key.

Sadly, you can't find a standard for these **FN** keys and their functions in the laptop world. But among the many laptops out there, you can find FN key combinations that do the following:

- Turn the laptop's internal speaker volume up and down.
- Mute the laptop's internal speaker.
- Increase or decrease the monitor's brightness or contrast.
- Activate an external monitor for giving a presentation.
- Lock the keyboard.

These functions are displayed as icons on the Function **(FN)** key bar.

Introduction

Function (FN) Keys Bar

This bar gets its name from the function **(FN)** keys it represents. For each button on this bar there is a corresponding function key that performs the same action. This bar is derived from the design of the first twin-panel file managers and the FN keys usually act the same way.

The FN key is usually placed either to the right or to the left of the left control key. In the latter case, it displaces the control key from the lower left corner of the keyboard. This is where the control key sits on keyboards without the FN key.

To display the FN key bar just press and hold the FN key and select the corresponding function key for the action required.

Activating a second function assigned to a dual-purpose key, the Fn key works like a shift key. For example, the F1 key is a dual-purpose key that controls laptop security . When FN is held down and F1 is pressed, the ordinary F1 key locks your computer.

Take a moment to peruse your laptop and look over the FN keys available. You may find some FN keys handy for various functions depending on your common usage, alternatively play around with them and see what you find.